Refugees

WORLD ISSUES

BookLife

Harriet Brundle

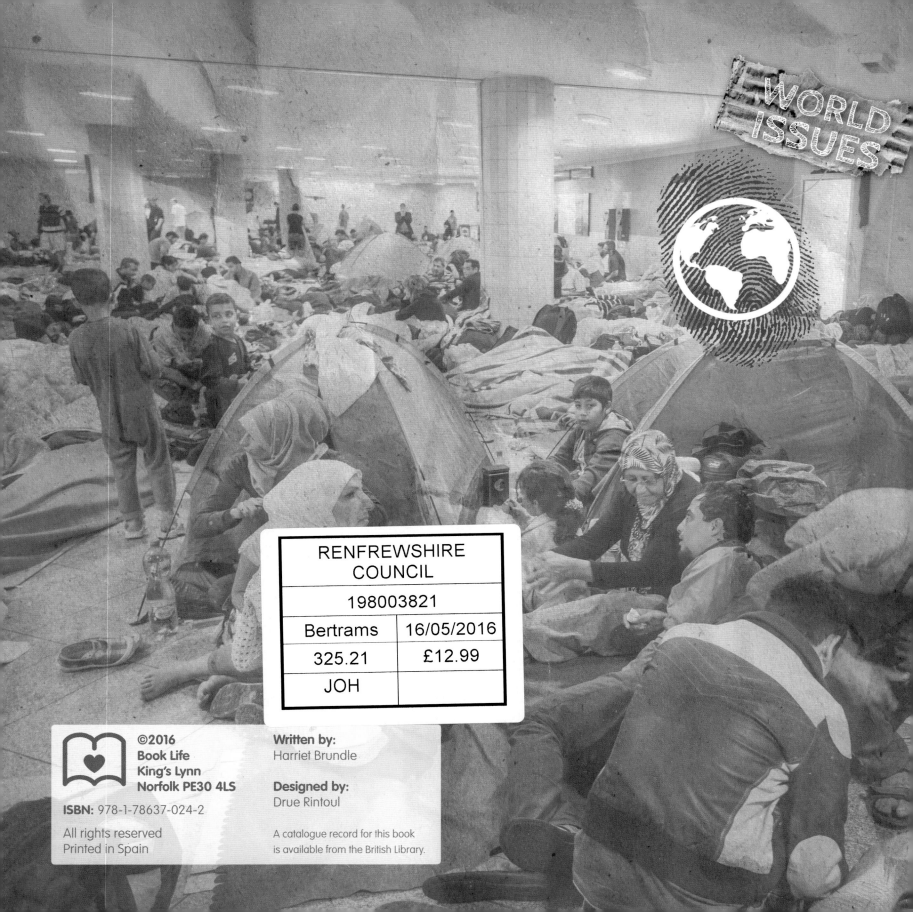

WORLD ISSUES

©2016
Book Life
King's Lynn
Norfolk PE30 4LS

ISBN: 978-1-78637-024-2

Written by:
Harriet Brundle

Designed by:
Drue Rintoul

A catalogue record for this book
is available from the British Library.

Contents

Words that look like *this* can be found in the Glossary on page 30.

Words that look like *this* are important words.

What is a Refugee?

A *refugee* is a person who has no choice but to leave their home country and is unable to return there. When a refugee has arrived in another country, they can apply for *asylum*, which means they will receive help from that country's government. Every person in the world has the right to seek asylum. A person waiting for their *asylum application* to be successful is called an *asylum seeker*.

A person who has had to leave their home, but has not moved to a different country, is referred to as an **Internally Displaced Person**.

Migration means to move from one place to another.

4

The government of a country will know how many refugees are seeking asylum by the number of asylum applications it receives; however, this number is not totally accurate, as not every refugee will claim asylum.

Asylum applications in 2014:

Germany
202, 815

France
64, 310

UK
31, 945

A refugee should claim asylum in the first safe country they reach. If a refugee is refused asylum by a country's government, they will not be able to live in that country. Sometimes, a refugee may choose to stay in that country after they have been refused, or will not inform the government when they arrive. In this case, they are an ***illegal immigrant***.

Why do People become Refugees?

A person becomes a refugee when they have claimed asylum in another country in order to escape from **persecution**, war or **natural disaster** in their home country. These events often destroy homes or make people feel unsafe. Due to this, people leave their home country, hoping to find a safer place to live.

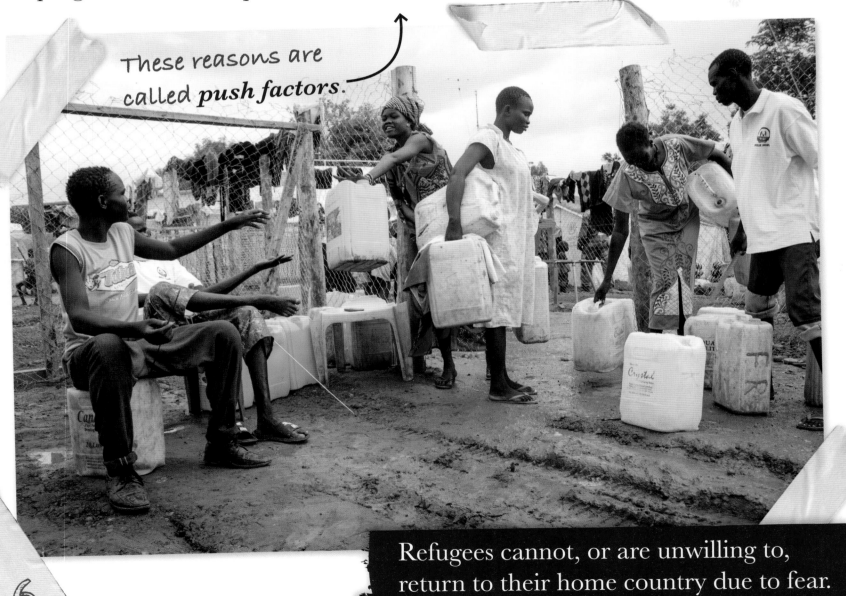

These reasons are called *push factors*.

Refugees cannot, or are unwilling to, return to their home country due to fear.

Over half the refugees in the world have come from just three countries which are Afghanistan, Syria and Somalia. Both Afghanistan and Syria have been effected by long term war which has left many people with no choice but to leave. Somalian people have suffered from drought, famine and unrest in their country.

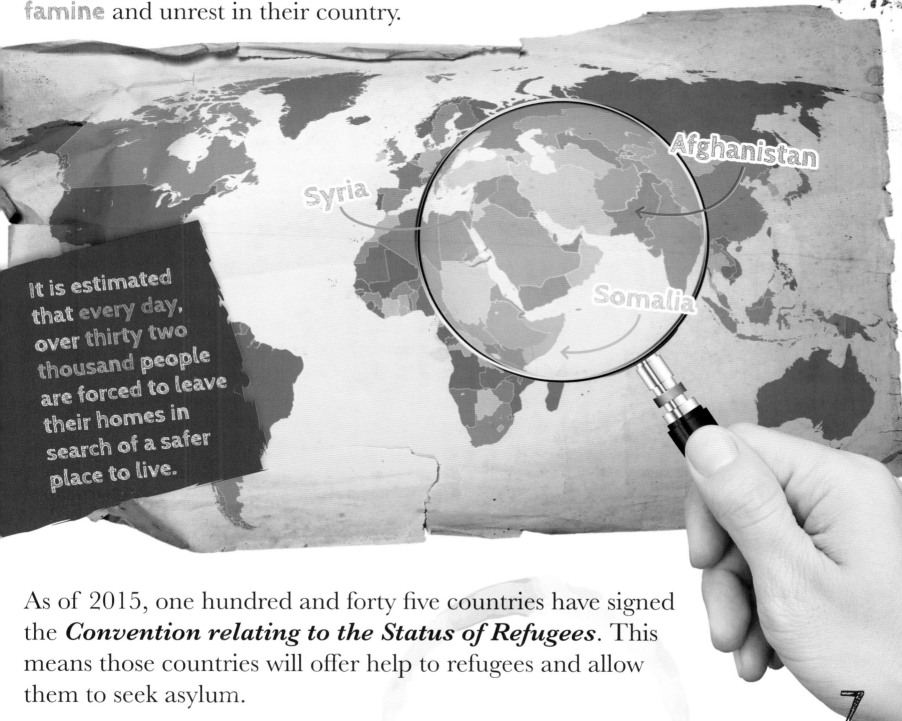

It is estimated that every day, over thirty two thousand people are forced to leave their homes in search of a safer place to live.

As of 2015, one hundred and forty five countries have signed the **Convention relating to the Status of Refugees**. This means those countries will offer help to refugees and allow them to seek asylum.

How do People Migrate?

Refugees often have no choice but to leave their home unexpectedly. They often have very little time to gather their belongings, plan their journey or organise a place to stay in a new country. Many refugees travel on foot, by boat and in vehicles, carrying their possessions with them. These journeys are extremely dangerous but sometimes this is the only option for refugees to reach a new home.

"I had no choice, I wanted to reach a place where I could fulfil my dreams and live in safety" – Mohammed.

Sadly, hundreds of refugees have died trying to reach a new country by these methods.

In desperate need to reach a new country, many refugees pay money to *smugglers* who transport them across country boarders by land, sea or air. The amount of money the refugees must pay depends on the distance they need to travel and the difficulty of the journey.

The money refugees pay may also include the cost of *illegal documents* they might need to cross into a country.

The smuggling of people is illegal and is extremely dangerous for the refugees themselves. Thousands of refugees have died whilst being transported in this way.

Refugee Camps

A *refugee camp* is a temporary place for refugees to live, until they find a permanent home. As the camps are only meant to be used for a short time, they are very basic. Camps are usually overcrowded, there is often not enough food or water. They can also be unclean which can result in refugees becoming extremely unwell.

It is not unusual for thousands of people to be staying in a refugee camp at one time.

Refugee camps are usually set up by a government or a charity, for example the Red Cross.

10

The Zaatari refugee camp in the country of Jordan was set up in 2012 and is the largest refugee camp in the Middle East. It is estimated that over eighty thousand people live in the camp; they have fled from the ongoing war in neighbouring country Syria.

"Here, we don't have friends. We used to go to school, but it is too far from here in the camp."
- Lama al-Absi

Zaatari was first built in just nine days and there have been many problems with the camp. These include a lack of electricity, water, shelter and healthcare. Only one in three children living at the camp receives an education. As the homes are only meant to be temporary, many people are living in tents, or small tin sheds with little furniture.

Migration *on Foot*

Many refugees have no choice but to undertake parts of their journey to a new country on foot. Most refugees carry their belongings with them and the journeys made can be tens or even hundreds of miles long. Many families have elderly people and young children with them who find the long journey even more difficult.

"We will walk 'till we drop. We have suffered so this is just another stop along the way."
Musa Hal

Parts of the journey on foot may be via dangerous routes, such as on busy roads or along train tracks. Many refugees have nowhere to stay while they are travelling so they have no choice but to sleep outside on the ground.

Thousands of refugees have made a journey of over one hundred miles from the city of Budapest in Hungary to the Austrian border on foot. Refugees who make this long journey are hoping to cross through Austria and reach Germany and other North Western European countries.

The journey the refugees take is extremely dangerous. Many have walked along the motorway and train tracks.

Refugees arrive in Hungary from Turkey and many are held for several days in refugee camps with little food or water. Many refugees don't want to stay in Hungary because they feel countries such as Germany are more developed and are more welcoming. In September 2015, a growing frustration due to lack of help from the Hungarian Government led thousands of refugees to break out from the camps and make the journey on foot to Austria.

Migration *by Boat*

To reach a new country, many refugees travel by boat across dangerous seas. They often sail in small, unsteady wooden or rubber boats which are unsuitable for long journeys across rough seas.

"Even if I knew the boat was going to sink, I would still have made the journey". Firas

In 2015, it was estimated that three hundred and fifty thousand people have reached Europe by sea. Sadly, hundreds of refugees died while trying to make the journey.

The boats are usually overcrowded, so the extra weight puts the boats under strain, causing them to sink or break. Small boats may be overturned in rough tides, resulting in tragedy for the passengers.

Many countries and charities have stepped in to offer help to refugees who have attempted to make part of their journey by boat. Lifeguard ships, government boats and even everyday fishermen have saved refugees who are in danger from drowning.

The United Nations Refugee Agency, also known as UNHCR, was set up to protect and help refugees. The agency has been working to encourage all governments to offer help to refugees who are making dangerous journeys across the sea.

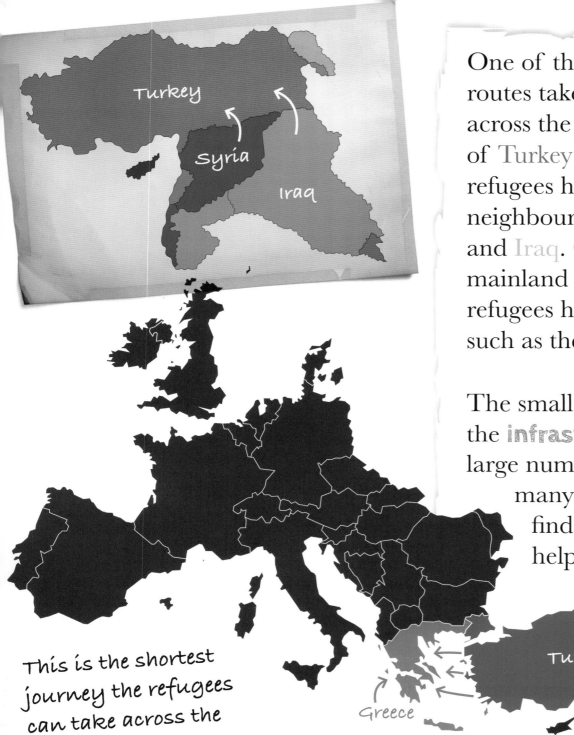

One of the most **frequently** used routes taken by refugees, is to travel across the Aegean Sea from the shores of Turkey to the Greek Islands. The refugees have arrived in Turkey from neighbouring countries such as Syria and Iraq. Once they have reached mainland Greece, many of the refugees hope to travel to countries such as the UK and Germany.

The small Greek Islands do not have the **infrastructure** to deal with the large numbers of people and so many of the refugees cannot find shelter and do not receive help from the government.

This is the shortest journey the refugees can take across the water if they want to reach Europe.

Number of refugees arriving in Greece:

2014 – 35,000

2015 – 234,000

Many other refugees are crossing the Mediterranean Sea, from North Africa across the water to Italy. Zuwara, on the coast of Libya, has become a popular place for refugees to depart from.

Italy

Libya

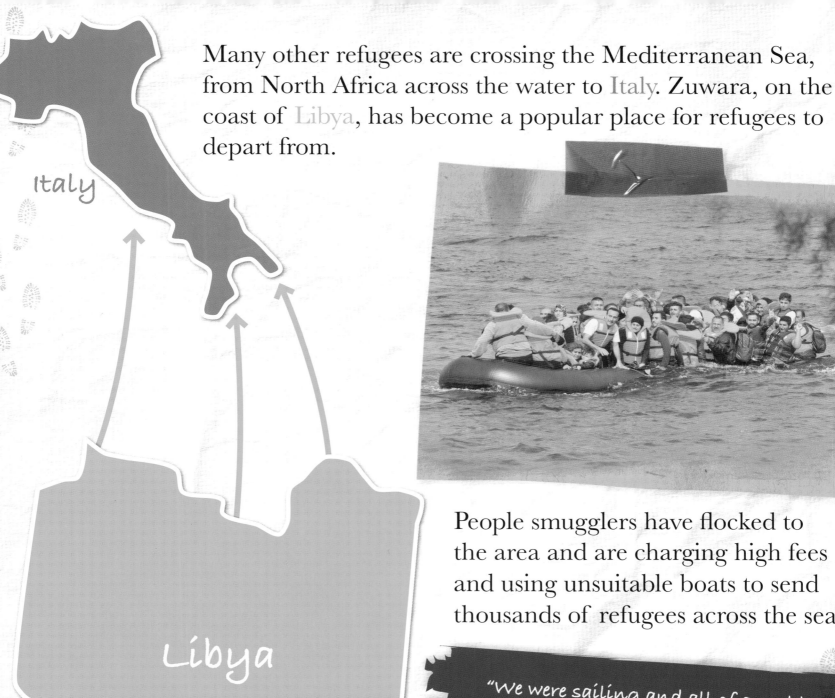

People smugglers have flocked to the area and are charging high fees and using unsuitable boats to send thousands of refugees across the sea.

"We were sailing and all of a sudden, the boat sank. Everyone on board died, except three or four people... The boat was not strong enough for such conditions."
Mohammed Alawi

Migration *by Vehicle*

Many refugees are attempting to enter countries such as the UK inside lorries and cars. While at a standstill, refugees climb inside the lorry container and hide there until reaching their destination.

Sadly, seventy one people were found dead inside a lorry in Austria in 2015; it is thought they were refugees from Syria.

People smugglers and drivers are illegally charging refugees money for a space inside the container; however, travelling inside a lorry is extremely dangerous. The refugees have very little space and the containers are often sealed so the people inside are cut off from fresh air.

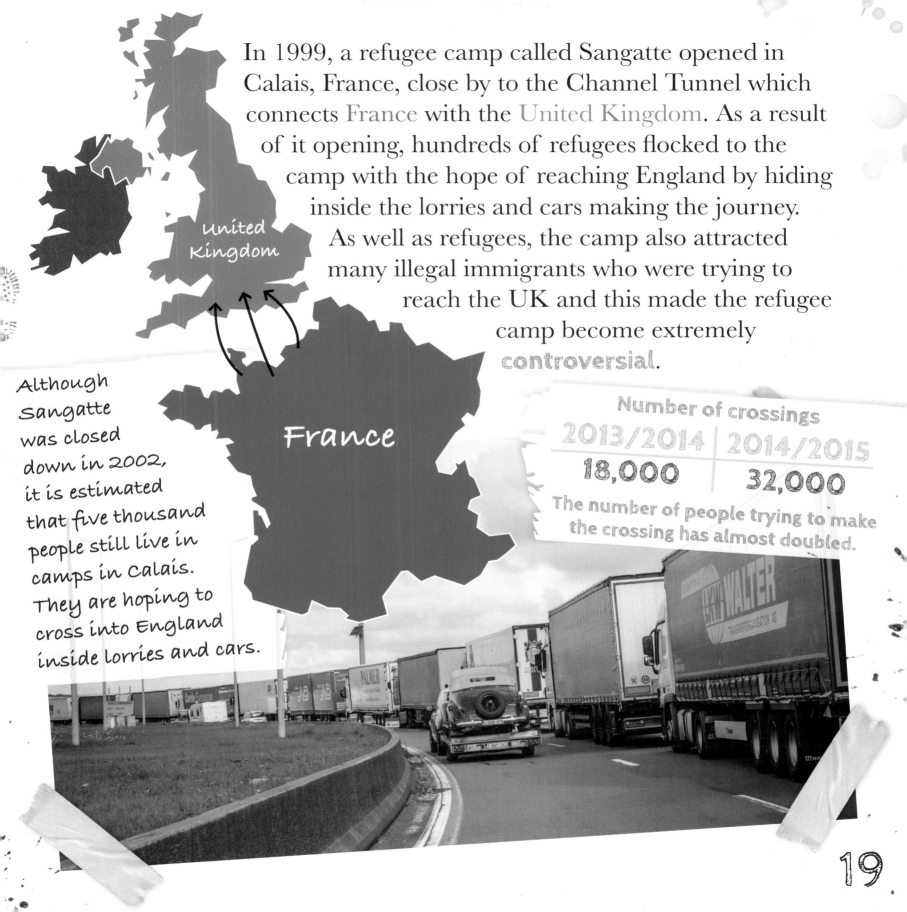

In 1999, a refugee camp called Sangatte opened in Calais, France, close by to the Channel Tunnel which connects France with the United Kingdom. As a result of it opening, hundreds of refugees flocked to the camp with the hope of reaching England by hiding inside the lorries and cars making the journey. As well as refugees, the camp also attracted many illegal immigrants who were trying to reach the UK and this made the refugee camp become extremely controversial.

United Kingdom

France

Although Sangatte was closed down in 2002, it is estimated that five thousand people still live in camps in Calais. They are hoping to cross into England inside lorries and cars.

Number of crossings	
2013/2014	2014/2015
18,000	32,000

The number of people trying to make the crossing has almost doubled.

How Does it Feel to be a Refugee?

For refugees, the journey to a new home can be extremely frightening. The journey itself is very dangerous and refugees may not be able to afford food or water, or find shelter. They may also have been separated from their friends and family, which is extremely distressing. Refugees may have loved ones who are still living in their home country and they do not know if they are alive.

"We have never lived like this before. We feel like we are dying slowly." Karzan

Those who are living in a refugee camp often have arrived with few belongings and are living in **unfurnished**, temporary accommodation. Many camps are so overcrowded that illness can spread extremely quickly. The refugees feel desperate to move on from the camps to find a safer and more permanent home.

When refugees arrive in a new country, it can be very difficult to begin with. They may have arrived in a country where people speak a different language and so they cannot understand what others are saying. This is called a **language barrier**. A language barrier can also make it difficult to make new friends.

These are called **cultural differences**.

Many refugees may want to wear a style of clothing that is traditional within their religion or home country; however, these clothes may look very different to the clothing worn by others who live in the new country.

In a new country, there may be food that refugees may not previously have eaten.

21

How do Others Feel about Refugees?

Lots of people feel differently about the best way to help refugees, so it is often talked about by governments and in the news. Some people feel that richer countries should help larger numbers of refugees. Others feel their country does not have the resources to be able to help, and therefore, the number of refugees allowed to enter should be limited.

Many refugees are of a working age, which has a positive effect on a country. Refugees who are working will earn money and therefore pay taxes, which help to fund public services such as the police force.

Each country has their own policy on refugees, so the number of people accepted is different for every country.

The German Chancellor, Angela Merkel, had an 'open door policy' with regard to the number of refugees the country would accept. In 2015, Germany were expecting a total of one and a half million refugees to arrive in the country.

It has been reported that thousands of German people helped to welcome refugees by providing blankets and food, and by teaching the refugees to understand and speak German.

Some people in Germany reacted badly to the volume of refugees arriving and felt the numbers should be limited. There were protests by German people and the police found it difficult to establish those who were refugees and those who should not have been entering the country.

Refugee Laws

International Refugee Law is mostly made up of the 1951 United Nations Convention Relating to the Status of Refugees and the 1967 Protocol Relating to the Status of Refugees. These laws were made to define what it means to be a refugee and to offer help and protection to refugees.

In order to qualify as a refugee and therefore be protected by refugee law, a person must meet very specific criteria. These include being outside of their country of origin and having a well-founded fear of persecution if they return to that country.

If a person fulfils the criteria, it is illegal for them to be returned to the country in which their life would be at risk. This is called the principle of **non-refoulement**.

In the UK, it is extremely difficult to be granted ***refugee status*** by law and many asylum applications are rejected. If an application is rejected, the person can appeal. If the appeal is unsuccessful, the person must leave the country.

In 2014, the UK received over thirty one thousand asylum applications.

Most people who have been recognised as refugees by law are only granted permission to stay in the UK for five years and are told this can be reviewed and changed at any time. This can make it extremely difficult for refugees to plan ahead in terms of work, family and owning their own home.

Case Study: Syria

Problems began in Syria in early 2011, when Syrian people began protesting against the actions of President Bashar al-Assad and demanded his **resignation**. By the middle of 2011, the protesters had taken up arms to protect themselves against security forces and as the violence increased, **civil war** started.

Since the war began other groups, including Islamic State, have become involved in the fighting and have claimed control of large parts of the country.

The civil war between those who supported President Assad and those who did not became increasingly violent and between 2011 and 2014, one hundred and ninety one thousand people were killed.

As a result of the violence across the country, more than four million people have fled from Syria and millions of others have been internally displaced. Buildings and homes have been destroyed and previously bustling towns and cities have been turned to rubble. Important buildings such as hospitals and schools have also been demolished.

"At first, we got used to the bullets and the fighting, but then the planes started bombing us. We never knew if we were safe." Hassan

Many of the Syrian refugees have moved to nearby countries, such as Turkey, Jordan and Iraq, while others hope to seek safety in Europe.

27

Quick Quiz

1. What is a refugee?

2. What does it mean if a person is an asylum seeker?

3. Name one sea that refugees are travelling across to reach safety.

4. What is a language barrier?

5. What is a refugee camp?

6. What is the principle of non-refoulement?

7. What are cultural differences?

Activity

Read each of the below and write down or discuss your answers:

Think about a time when you have left your home, for example going on holiday. What items did you take with you and why?

What would you take with you if you only had a few minutes to pack your belongings?

Think about how you would feel if you could never go back to your home. Where would you go? How would you get there?

Glossary

Civil War – a war fought between people who live in the same country

Controversial – something that causes public disagreement

Criteria – a standard by which something is judged

Drought – a long period of little or no rain water

Famine – when there is not enough food for a large number of people

Frequently – often

Infrastructure – the basic services, such as power supply, that a country needs to function

Natural Disaster – a natural event, for example an earthquake, that causes great damage to an area

Origin – where a person was born

Permanent – something that lasts forever

Persecution – cruel or unfair treatment because of race, religion or political beliefs

Resignation – deciding to leave your job

Temporary – when something lasts for a short amount of time

Unfurnished – without any furniture

Index

Photo Credits

Photocredits: Abbreviations: l-left, r-right, b-bottom, t-top, c-centre, m-middle.
All images are courtesy of Shutterstock.com.

Front Coverm Procyk Radek.. bl & tr - Gilmanshin. 2 - Istvan Csak. 3tr - Lana Veshta. 3br - Gilmanshin. 4r - Procyk Radek. 4bl - jannoon028. 5m - Ververidis Vasilis. 6m - punghi. 7br -tanatat. 8m - Orlok . 9m - Malcolm Chapman. 10m - Sadik Gulec. 10bl - NRT. 11lm - Paskee. 11mr - dreibirnen. 12mr - Janossy Gergely. 12br - Volodymyr Borodin. 13ml - Janossy Gergely. 13tr - pavalena. 14m - punghi. 15m - Chat des Balkans. 17tr - Anjo Kan. 18m - Milos Muller. 19b - lumokajlinioj. 20ml - Ververidis Vasilis. 20mr - hikrcn. 21tr - Mila Supinskaya. 21b - Jag_cz. 22r - pcruciatti. 22bl - Oleksiy Mark. 23tl - 360b. 23ml - Spectral-Design. 23mr - Claudio Divizia. 24tl - Africa Studio. 24br - Photoman29. 25m - Prazis. 26r - Valentina Petrov. 26l - kc.bangkhew. 27tr - Orlok. 27m - Istvan Csak. 28tr - Brian A Smith. 29tr - BlueOrange Studio.

WORLD
ISSUES